Praise for

Winner of the Year 2001

"Beth Ann Fennelly's poems are consistently dramatic, complex in their perceptions and formal unfolding, and enthralled with language. . . . This is one of the most interesting, challenging, and accomplished first books to appear in recent years. . . . Genuinely outstanding." —*Harvard Review*

"Beth Ann Fennelly's *Open House* marks an auspicious debut. . . . Fennelly tempers cognitive power and sensual wordplay with a subversive wit born of wry self-knowledge."

—Floyd Collins, *Westbranch*

"Fennelly approaches language with playfulness and reverence, heady with possibilities, wary of dilution."

—Tim Rauschenberger, *Christian Science Monitor*

"These poems can be elegiac, passionate, meditative, tender, angry, and funny by turns. Beth Ann Fennelly is clearly a poet to watch."

—*Notre Dame Review*

"Riveting reading. . . . At a time when so many poets seem to think it's uncool to be kind or sincere, one is thankful for Fennelly's heart." —*Borderlands: Texas Poetry Review*

"Decidedly ambitious. . . . Fennelly, by the end of *Open House*, has done much to widen our definition of what poetry can be."

—Denise Duhamel, *Painted Bride Quarterly*

"An essential collection from a truly gifted writer." —*First Draft*

"Some poetry books are energetic. Some are elegant. Some are broad, some deep. Some are generous, some personal, some universal. Occasionally the reader finds a poetry book that is all of these and more. Such a book is Beth Ann Fennelly's *Open House*."
—*Birmingham Poetry Review*

"[Fennelly's] poems are as playful as they are thoughtful and conscientious in their wordplay. They are every bit as vulnerable and honest as they are ambitious." —*Crab Orchard Review*

"Fennelly [is] a poet with range. Also apparent is her quick sense of humor. She is deft with form . . . she risks moving boldly toward sentimentality and nostalgia without slipping into wither."
—*Mid-American Review*

"Fennelly invents a whole new architecture to house the many voices of her rich imagination." —*Valparaiso Poetry Review*

"*Open House*, for all its discursive play, achieves a thematic breadth and range of emotion, and signals the emergence of a poet of liveliness and depth." —*Gulf Coast*

Also by Beth Ann Fennelly

Unmentionables

Great with Child:
Letters to a Young Mother

Tender Hooks

OPEN HOUSE

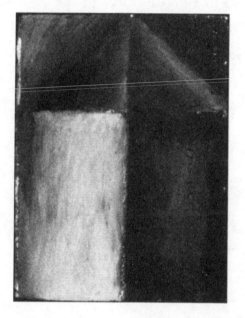

POEMS BY
BETH ANN FENNELLY

W.W. Norton & Company

New York • London

Copyright © 2002 by Beth Ann Fennelly

First published as a Norton paperback 2009

For information about permission to reproduce selections from this book,
write to Permissions, W. W. Norton & Company, Inc.,
500 Fifth Avenue, New York, NY 10110

For information about special discounts for bulk purchases, please contact
W. W. Norton Special Sales at specialsales@wwnorton.com or 800-233-4830

Manufacturing by Courier Westford
Production manager: Devon Zahn

Library of Congress Cataloging-in-Publication Data

Fennelly, Beth Ann –
   Open house : poems / by Beth Ann Fennelly.— 1st ed.
      p. cm.
   ISBN 0-9708177-5-4
   I. Title.
   PS3556.E489 O64 2002
   811'.54—dc21
zoo004

ISBN 978-0-393-33607-8 pbk.

W. W. Norton & Company, Inc.
500 Fifth Avenue, New York, N.Y. 10110
www.wwnorton.com

W. W. Norton & Company Ltd.
Castle House, 75/76 Wells Street, London W1T 3QT

1 2 3 4 5 6 7 8 9 0

Acknowledgments

Grateful acknowledgment is made to the editors of the following journals in which these poems originally appeared: *Arts & Letters, The American Scholar, The Carolina Quarterly, Columbia, The Gettysburg Review, The Kenyon Review, The Michigan Quarterly Review, The Notre Dame Review, Poetry Ireland Review, Poetry Northwest, TriQuarterly,* and *Shenandoah.*

Poems from this collection were reprinted in: *The Best American Poetry 1996; The Book of Irish American Poetry from the Eighteenth Century to the Present; Contemporary American Poetry; Line Drives: 100 Contemporary Baseball Poems; Lineas Connectadas: Nueva Poesia de los Estados Unidos; Literature: A Pocket Anthology; The Penguin Book of the Sonnet; Poets of the New Century; Poetry Daily; The Pushcart Prize: Best of the Small Presses, 2001;* and *Thirteen Ways of Looking for a Poem.*

For my mother and my sister, who could author books called *Loyalty* and *Love*;

For my husband, *more than friends* now and forever;

And for our daughter, Claire.

Contents

On Fennelly's *Open House*   xiii
   by David Baker

I. The Room of Dead Languages

The Impossibility of Language   3
The Names of Things   8
Mother Sends My Poem to Her Sister with Post-Its   10
Poem Not to Be Read at Your Wedding   11
The Insecurities of Great Men   12
The Cup Which My Father Hath Given Me   13

II. The Room of Echoes

Mary Speaks to the Early Visitor at the Laying Out   19
Letter from Gauguin's Daughter   23
Asked for a Happy Memory of Her Father, She Recalls
         Wrigley Field   25
Yield   26
Madame L. Describes the Siege of Paris   27

III. The Room of Paper Walls

From *L' Hôtel Terminus Notebooks*   33

IV. The Room of Everywhere

The Snake Charmer   65
Why I Can't Cook for Your Self-Centered Architect
         Cousin   66
I Would Like to Go Back as I Am, Now, to You as You Were,
         Then—   68
Good Work if You Can Get It   70
Come to Krakow   73

Notes   75

On Fennelly's *Open House*

Beth Ann Fennelly's *Open House* is a brilliant blueprint of the imagination. But where George Herbert shaped his literary architecture into a holy temple, and where E. A. Poe peered through the smudged windows of the House of Usher to find a decaying subconscious, this exciting new poet throws open all her doors to admit whoever and whatever is in shouting range. I am drawn gladly to the inclusiveness, the intellectual size, the contagious play in Fennelly's work, and to her extraordinary range of her styles, tones, and forms.

At the center of *Open House* is a superb long poem, "From *L'Hotel Terminus Notebooks*." Midway through the poem itself, one character, Mr. Daylater, teases the poem's protagonist and speaker, Beth Ann, with his gentle ribbing: "You have a lot of friends. Some of whom even exist." Mr. D. serves here as the poet's alter ego—companion, nag, fellow esthete, and something of a trickster—and is himself one of the vivid if fictive characters he refers to, one of the teeming populace of Fennelly's book. This particular poem-as-notebook shimmers with imaginative energy, less a lyric monologue than a Greek play full of voices and chorus-like accompaniments. "I sing of the four categories from which art is drawn," our poet croons, invoking her muses while she winks at us. The poem is a performance of Fennelly's processes of inheritance and fabrication. Blending the postmodern and the ancient, she "search[es] the system" of her mind's mainframe to ">Retrieve: "god, gods, goddess, god-like"; she traces the mating habits of African bowerbirds; she makes lists, takes notes, and stews over the etymology of words, the idiosyncrasies of Frank Lloyd Wright—all to explicate the making, the building of a poem.

"From *L'Hotel Terminus Notebooks*" may be the main chamber in *Open House*, but a number of other passages and rooms radiate from its center. In one section, "The Room of Dead Languages," the poet broods with aesthetic anxiety—self-conscious and revealing—in the manner of Robert Hass or Wallace Stevens. In another section, "The Room of Echoes," we find a series of dramatic monologues, powerfully spoken, ranging historically from Milton's death chamber to Gauguin's Copenhagen to Wrigley Field. How many young poets can claim both Browning and Hass as their rhetorical forebears?

Fennelly's curiosity and learning belie her young age. She is as inclusive and playful as Albert Goldbarth, stacking references to Harlequin-romance guidelines alongside the Siege of Paris, tracing the idiom for a hangover in different languages ("In Czech, 'The monkeys swing inside my head'") while recreating the menu of a death-row inmate's last meal. She can spread a poem wide as a notebook or make it terse as a post-it note; she constructs lovely sonnets and syllabics, measures her monologues in graceful blank verse, and yet can unleash a heady, raucous tangle of language unbounded by lines or polite manners. For all the range and variety, though, central to these poems is a coherent, complex sense of self and that self's evolving relation to culture, family, and work.

Beth Ann Fennelly's *Open House* stands out from the poetry of most younger American poets with their sober self-confessions or, conversely, their sarcastic throw-away wit. Here is sincere passion in great, mature portions, a tenderness toward her characters both far away and near, a historical aptitude and relevance, a strength of spirit, and a wisdom at home in the substantial body of the work. I greet this book, this poet, with joy.

—David Baker, series judge and poetry editor of
The Kenyon Review

I. The Room of Dead Languages

The Impossibility of Language

1.

"Blackberries," says one, rolling it in the barrel
of the mouth. "Yes," says the other, "oak."
"Well aged, aroma of truffles," adds the third.
They nod. Discuss the legs of it running
down the glass. They roll it and roll it, the way
God must have packed the earth in his palms.
They bring the valley into it. And color: "The light
staining the glass at Sainte Chapelle." Back to taste:
"Earthy. A finish of clove." They leave nodding—
such faith in the opaque bottles of their words.

2. How I Became a Nature Lover

Suppose I said, "Honeysuckle,"
meaning stickysweet stamen,
the hidden core you taught me,
a city girl, to find. How I crave
the moment I coax it from calyx,
tongue under bulbed tip
of glistening stalk, like an altar boy
raising the salver under the blessed bread
the long Sundays of my girlhood,
suppose my tongue caught that mystery,
that   single   swollen   drop
                    O
              honey-
              suckle

The irony of metaphor:
you are closest to something
when naming what it's not.

3

3.

1934: Imagine Mandelstam, who loved words
recklessly, with his poet friends,
how they passed the bottle of slivovicé.
"Osip," they pleaded, "chitáy, chitáy."
And so he did read about Stalin,
"the Kremlin mountaineer," with "laughing
cockroaches on his top lip" who rolled
"executions on his tongue like berries."
How could Mandelstam have known
one man fisting the table in laughter
would quote the poem to the mountaineer?

Think of Mandelstam in winter: the water
freezes in the water jug. In summer:
the prison mattress shimmies lice.
But his wife, Nadezhda, visits him.
They do not speak of hope or love or death.
He recites his poems in a whisper
that she memorizes. Even in his cell,
"this shoe-size in earth with bars around it,"
as long as he has lips, he has a weapon.

Imagine how much each word weighs
on Nadezhda's tongue. She bears them
home like eggs in that time of no eggs.
She nests them deep inside the secret book.
He dies, committed to her memory.

4.

"I ask you to cinema, coffee, wine,
          you say me, 'no.' I ask you
walk of the park, hold of the hand.
          You say me, 'no.' You gave my heart

the fire, and now you give me the heart
        burn. Why, when eyes of you
hold the sympathy like some fox?"
        We speak barest when we barely
speak—love letters from the foreigner
        before the invention of cliché.

Teaching immigrants English,
        I gave them crayons to draw families,
taught them words for each brown,
        orange, tan face. Guillermo's page
was blank. "I am alonesome," he wrote.

5.

Meaning? Language can so not.

The government releases
films of nuclear testing
from the fifties.
A plane bellies over
an atoll in the Pacific.
It drops a bomb.
The camera,
at a "safe distance"
some dozen islands away,
flips over. The sky
falls. The narrator surmises,
"at this juncture
of maturation,
premature impactation
necessitates further study."
The mushroom cloud
is a balloon caption
for which earth
can't find
words.

6.

Is the ear bereft if an alphabet dies
that it has never heard?

> "The latest extinction of language
> occurred last month with the death
> of the lone speaker of Northern Pomo,
> a woman in her eighties."

Are we weaker without the word
in Northern Pomo for begonia?
Does the inner hammer numbly
strike its drum? Does it grow dumb
mourning sounds that it will never hear?

7. Unfinished Poems

rise
from trash cans
sewers & pulp mills
& bind themselves under
elaborate covers
for the endless library
of the unborn
who climb mahogany
ladders to finger
thick volumes
& with vague lips
sound out what's there
& what's not

8.

Synonyms are lies. Answer the question
with *stones* or *rocks*:

Q. When Virginia Woolf, on the banks
of the Ouse, walked into the water,
swallowing her words, with what objects
had she loaded the pockets of her dress?

A. *Stones. Rocks* is wrong, as in
"She took her life for granite."

9. The Myth of Translation

Try a simple sentence: "I am hungover."
For Japanese, "I suffer the two-day dizzies."
In Czech, "The monkeys swing inside my head."
Italians say, "Today, I'm out of tune."
Languages aren't codes that correspond—
in Arabic, there is no word for "hungover."

Does the Innuit wife, kept on ice all winter,
sucking fat from ducks for her hunter's leggings,
not divine the boredom her language doesn't name?
Or would the word's birth crack the ice for miles,
drowning the hunter who crouches with a spear
beside the ice hole for the bearded seal? She sucks
the fat slowly, careful not to quill her throat
with feathers. She grows heavy. It is, as it was
from the beginning, a question of knowledge.
If she bites into the word, she'll be alonesome.

The Names of Things

1.

Why? asks the Sears' security guard, but she can't
tell him about the names of colors in the lip gloss sampler
she's slipped inside her tote. She has no words to say
that the name *Ballerina Pink* is scruffed toe-shoes
stuffed with lambs wool and bleeding feet,
that *Boysenberry* draws boys to lips of ripening spring.

Soon she will be taken home, climb the long stairway
to her mother lying in the sick room of the girl's
entire childhood, because of the tragic Missed Carriage.
Sometimes the girl imagines a baby brother
held through the carriage window by sequined gloves.
Sometimes the school nuns produce the boy,
finger their heavy crosses before signaling the driver
to crunch on through the gravel. She can't ask why
her mother was late, or if this too was her father's fault—
her mother is "not to be pestered by precocious little girls."
You're a queer one," says the nurse. "Mind your p's and q's,"
the girl would have retorted if every day her father
didn't put three fingers to his lips and twist, throw the key
over his shoulder, like you do with spilt salt, no bad luck.

2.

The names of things will never lose their hold on her.
By now, her parents have surrendered. She knows
nothing of her history, must rediscover everything.
She starts with her name. From the Gaelic, "Fennelly"
means "fair warrior." Her mother's "McNamara":
"son of the hound of the sea." And there in the book:
"These two clans have been warring for centuries . . ."
The names, making it happen. Within, she is chanting

Tawny Peach, *Passionfruit*, smearing her lips *Cotton Candy*,
Black Coffee, staining her *Scarlet*, *Burnt Clay*,
and *Blood Red*—lubricants, but still a lip-locked girl.

Mother Sends My Poem to Her Sister with Post-Its

This man is an abstract
painter gives his women
one eye, three breasts
a very famous man

> She doesn't smoke
> anymore

> > a kind of cheese?

This woman is not me
she says even though
I used to ice skate
with Bill in a red
scarf in winter

> That's how the French
> girls got the silk
> from the worms, they
> dipped the cocoons
> in scalding tubs of water
> (13th c.)

> > this apple is a symbol

She got this wrong
it was me, not her father
who sang her "Irish Rosie"
she was so sick with the measles

> > When she writes "far gone
> > train" it means she plans
> > to come back home

Poem Not to Be Read at Your Wedding

You ask me for a poem about love
in place of a wedding present, trying to save me
money. For three nights I've lain
under glow-in-the-dark-stars I've stuck to the ceiling
over my bed. I've listened to the songs
of the galaxy. Well, Carmen, I would rather
give you your third set of steak knives
than tell you what I know. Let me find you
some other, store-bought present. Don't
make me warn you of stars, how they see us
from that distance as miniature and breakable
from the bride who tops the wedding cake
to the Mary on Pinto dashboards
holding her ripe, red heart in her hands.

The Insecurities of Great Men

It is a job for great men: to pack a space probe
   with what we do and love. To say to the infinite:
      "Here we are." Imagine the great men grown from boys
         who dreamed of hitting a ball so hard it never
            came back, a homer's wild ellipsis out in space.
        How did they decide what to include?
        Carl Sagan consulted his team of rocket scientists—
  even the blind physicist who's never seen a star,
but listens to their radio waves to catch any S. O. S.
   from the frizzy hiss of space. Naturally selected
      to represent us, here are the photos they chose
         for the probe: *eagles, sequoias, seashells, the sun,*
            the Great Wall, the Taj Mahal, a group of astronauts,
            and a stick figure pregnant woman.
        One wonders why this bare bones sketch,
      what part of pregnancy offends: the flaking
of colostrum from the darkened areolas,
     the white stitches on the stretching seams of skin,
        the linea nigra—dark track linking navel to genitalia,
         reminding even great men of that black hole
            from which they sprang? Or is it because
         she's an everyday miracle their studies fail to explain?
      Or again, the pure, non-Euclidean plane of her,
    the fuzzy math, the census taker's irritation
at She-who-is-more-than-she-is? Does the death rattle
   of some distant star give birth to more in them
      than a universe kick starting beneath her swollen fingers?
        Or is the substitution a concession to the delicacy
         of the aliens? Oh great men, how will those creatures
        R. S. V. P. when they circle in the wet grass
      where the probe has landed, belly up, slick
    with perspiration, moaning open in their arms,
yielding its precious issue with a gust of steam
   and rust into their holy and natural world,
      and a woman made of sticks unhinges in their hands?

The Cup Which My Father Hath Given Me

I. Turning Twenty-Nine

You thought by now you'd be wiser,
not still falling for the old x=y.
You wonder how you'd do if you were
the last person on earth and had to found
a new civilization: could you describe
how an engine works? A radio? A light bulb?
You repeat the word *bulb. Bulb, bulb, bulb.*
You stop in the nick of time. Time nicks us all
sooner or later, that's democracy.
Once you were in Russia and a woman
cut your hair. She bent you over a tub,
noosed you in a towel and snipped away.
It was the best cut you ever got.
You drank tumblers of vodka with her husband.
The next day, your last in that country,
you took a bus to the Hermitage
and puked in the john until closing.
You didn't see a painting. Not one.
Somehow, you're this kind of person.
It's hard to believe, though you were voted
Most Likely to Yak in Russia's Best Museum
with Good Hair. Don't you hate it
when high school's right? Don't you hate it
when 2nd person swishes its tongue inside your ear?
You wonder how you'd do in solitary confinement.
You can't do long division in your head.
You don't know isometric exercises.
Edison's last words: *It is beautiful over there.*
Yours: *These pretzels are making me thirsty.*
You wonder if suffering makes people
more compassionate. Coleridge, caring
for his typhoid son, wrote by candlelight
twenty-three nights into the fever:

Turned a poor (very large & beautiful)
Moth out of the Window in a hard Shower
of rain to save it from the Flames!
That's one kind of person.
When you visit your father who is dying
at last, and he turns, death-dumb,
and whispers, *Did you bring Beth Ann?*
You say, *No*. That's another.

II. My Father's Pregnancy

It was no false alarm. We barely got there in time. He had that
glow, a yellow one. His belly was swollen, his skull was promi-
nent, his eyes bulged like two yolks. Beside him on the hospi-
tal night stand there was a cheap vase filled with droopy, father-
colored daffodils that someone had been overcharged for.
Hooked to IVs and monitors, knowing the end was near, he was
beatific, had labored toward this, pressed his hot mouth to the
slick O of his love, consuming it, swallowing, swallowing,
grown sick with desire. He lost the will to conceal, taking it at
work, in the car. He must have known how this would end—
the whispering neighbors, the elaborate cover ups, the family
trying to interfere, him at last sneaking away to wait it out
alone. So there couldn't have been much surprise when it
planted itself in his body. The delicate slug of his liver speck-
led and festered. The other mossy organs curled aside so it
could grow. And this brave father, tinting pollen-yellow, carried
it to term; he endured the thin nights of sleep, the mornings of
vomit and headaches, the clumsiness, the weakening bladder,
the body not quite his alone anymore. Toward the end, all he
could stomach was a mouthful or two of ice cream. But my
father had fidelity. It was the greatest love he had ever known,
and even then, he had no remorse. He was groaning, we were
counting his breaths, he was bearing down.

III. Cremains

I've made you ugly   as you never were in life,
      this tacky word, this
            neologism you'd have hated.
I've burned your beautiful body
to rubble, Dad,
           burned you until you rattle, a jar of mar-
bles
a child could scatter,
     a pile
          to be swept under the rug,
       or sneezed to the four winds,
                       I've seen to it
that nothing will bloom
            after rooting in your rich loam.
No stone
with your name that's my name.   No home.

      Yet there's the matter of matter.
Even now
       you are sifting over Vienna,
               powdering the para-
sols.
Even now you are snuffing
            the dog curled at his master's
feet
      beside a workbench in Pompei.
Even now
       you have come close, closer—
                the ash that apes
      what once was there,   massing
   at the end of my husband's cigar
              unsealed
from its glass coffin,
         thrust   into the fire

II. The Room of Echoes

Mary Speaks to the Early Visitor at the Laying Out

You're welcome here, kind sir, take off your cloak.
It seems you've traveled far to pay respects—
a friend from Cambridge? No? Well, never mind.
Anne, Deborah, and I have baked the day
and you shall be refreshed, though father died
and left us, orphaned, with the larder bare.
Yes, you're right. He'd taken a third wife—
three wives and three daughters, he loved
his trinities. So no, we're not quite orphans,
the wife is here to share my share of naught.
Have a glass of elderberry wine?

I'm pleased you like it, we made it ourselves
for men who came to meet the famous author.
Not that he'd have a glass—water alone
passed his lips the three and twenty years
I've been on earth. He was not a man
for simple pleasures. He'd forget to eat.
When Deb and I read him the Hebrew Bible—
(we didn't know the languages but learned
to sound the words) we'd find we needed more
than vowels to chew. "Can we eat our gruel?"
He'd raise his blind, bleared eyes in our direction.
I daresay that he now enjoys the cotton
that's puffing out his lips as much as joint
of mutton.

                Well, yes, I'll tell what happened,
despite my lack of skill at giving speeches—
I haven't had much practice. Our mother died
while laboring; she took with her the boy
inside her. Papa, longing for a son,
soon met a second wife who stayed two months,

that's all, then fled home to her mother. He found,
regarding marriage, our King and Church are wrong—
divorce is right, divorce should be allowed.
He published pamphlets saying so, which brought
the censor and his torch. The smell of burning words
still lingers in this house, at least for me.
Thereafter Papa weakened, gnarled with goiter.
He cursed—I heard him—at the doctor's order:
choose between the inkpot and your eyes.
He worked for six more months in black and white
so lived his last twelve years without a sunset.

We sisters went to Pinkham's School for Charm.
Deborah sang like one of Papa's angels.
I was fringing pillows, tatting lace.
The eldest one is Anne—she's lame, but sweet,
and could have been a curate's wife at least.
(We were of the age to think of marriage.)
But Papa called us home to be his readers.
He rose at four. Which meant we rose at four.
We'd lead him to his seat before the fire:
"Girls," he'd say, "I need my morning milking."
He'd recite new lines, our hands worked fast
to yank them into pails of parchment paper.
When he was empty, he would have us read.
We got to where we could sound out Italian,
Latin, Hebrew, Spanish, French, and Greek.

This went on for years. We'd copy down
"Doth God exact Day-labour, light denied?"
We wondered if God factored who comprised
the labour. Artillery Walk was kept barren
of suitors; Papa drove us from the parlor
when men came there to talk of politics
or hear how he met aged Galileo.
Andrew Marvell once spied me in the kitchen
but Papa said, "She's my amanuensis."
Which put an end to that.

                         It worsened.
He felt his days were few. He'd wake with sonnets
screaming in his head, scream them at ours.
Sometimes I'd just pretend to write them down.
It got so that he'd stop to feel my hand,
the page I'd carved with doodles, then resume.
He kept us up all night to write of Samson,
"Eyeless in Gaza at the mill with slaves."
We saw the parallels, but we, not him,
would brace in doorways dreaming of the push
that'd cave the house. At last, one birdless Monday:
"I'm dying," he moaned. "The earth shall roll in flames."
He did, but it did not, praised be the Lord.

That was three days ago. The layer out
then bathed his body, strapped him to a board,
and tied his legs so his soul couldn't walk.
His fingers, blue and bent, formed fists so tight
we kept them straight by fixing them to sticks.
We tied his goitered chin so Lucifer
and witches couldn't coven on his tongue.
We placed fresh minted pennies on the eyes
that nevermore would see they couldn't see.

Most lacking where most needed, dignity
was not an honored guest at Papa's death.
Our narrow staircase twisting to the parlor
could not accommodate my Papa's board.
We tried it high and low and on its side.
We lowered him, at last, from the bow window.
Neighbors got some ropes, I went below.
If I live to be sixty-six like him
I never will see a stranger sight: Papa
swinging into sunshine, wings of gauze
aflap his shoulders, bed sheets billowing.
Descending from the sun, he blinded me.
I wept, which I did not expect to do.

That's the story best as I can tell it.
I'd like to sleep late but still wake at four,
my tongue outstretched where Babel has been razed.
We've sold his library to pay his debts
and bought Deborah that harpsichord inside.
Well, sir, you may enter at your leisure.
We're grateful for your visit, but I didn't
hear your name.
        Peter? That is strange,
in "Lycidas," St. Pet—well, never mind.
You've come for Papa, he's laid out within.
If you chance to pass this way again,
you'd be welcome, sir. Perhaps some whist?
You could be our fourth, if you desire.
We plan to keep a lively parlor now.

Letter from Gauguin's Daughter

Papa,
      Enclosed is what little money
your last exhibition made here in Copenhagen.
Please do not be discouraged; the light in this city
is so muted, not even snow can be white.
Your flat impasto of magenta, of orange—
of course the reviewers would see it as caricature.

You ask about our health. Mother is not improved.
In her fever she forgets our reversal of fortune,
the exile from Paris. She dreams of our house
on the rue de Lorette, asks if you're home from the bank,
or at your Sunday hobby, painting that cute red fox?
Bedridden, she rings me to describe Paris
from her window above these rotting Danish docks.

I am well, besides missing you and France.
Every day my Danish aunts introduce me
to the blond eyelashes of some local Lars or Søren
who seeks a hard working wife. I suppose
I should be grateful, being twenty-seven and too thin.
Yes, I still sketch when I'm home from work
at the seamstress', and I'm glad you think
I capture well the harpsichord in the parlor.

Papa, it's five years since you left us here,
telling me *care for mother*, telling me *six months*.
But you paint someone called *Vahinè*, who sits
with earth-tipped breasts, weaving a basket
from screw pine. On her blanket is the pipe
you'd pack with cherry tobacco in the evenings.
Now your foxes are fanged and not so picturesque.

Just yesterday I looked in the pier glass, Papa,
and laughed to realize I'm still waiting

to get prettier, happier, waiting for my neck
to grow graceful before I wear my pearls.
But we stop growing, Papa, or most of us do.
I remember once, as a girl, walking into your studio—
I heard Mother's brassy bell, its note of need.
You stood painting, unhearing. On your easel,
a room with a window through which could be seen
the glad back of somebody walking away.

Papa, I must finish this letter. Yes,
you'll have money when the seamstress pays me.
What do you think of my sketches? Excuse me, the bell rings—

                              Aline

Asked for a Happy Memory of Her Father, She Recalls Wrigley Field

His drinking was different in sunshine,
as if it couldn't be bad. Sudden, manic,
he swung into a laugh, bought me
two ice creams, said *One for each hand.*

Half the hot inning I licked Good Humor
running down wrists. My bird-mother
earlier, packing my pockets with sun block,
has hopped her warning: *Be careful.*

So, pinned between his knees, I held
his Old Style in both hands
while he streaked the lotion on my cheeks
and slurred *My little Indian princess.*

Home run: the hairy necks of men in front
jumped up, thighs torn from gummy green bleachers
to join the violent scramble. Father
held me close and said *Be careful,*

be careful. But why should I be full of care
with his thick arm circling my shoulders,
with a high smiling sun, like a home run,
in the upper right-hand corner of the sky?

Yield

She makes them still, recipes serving eight
or ten or twelve. It's what she is, the stroganoff,
the lasagna. She bakes and rearranges
the cluttered fridge, the curdled quarts of milk,
bronze cold cuts oxidizing green, pork chops—
her husband's favorite. Sleepless, she bruises garlic
and pulls the beards from mussels. At the gargling
disposal: she marries ketchup from two family-
sized bottles. A habit. A necessary lie.

If there was ever a way to cook for one,
she can't remember, or who she was exactly
when she knew. Her babies, grown
and quarrel-scattered, come back only in dreams
to search the freezer, asking, "What is there to eat?"
She pleads, "I'll make you anything you want,"
then wakes, turns on the twelve-cup coffee pot.
She writes a list of what's gone bad, what's gone,
then shops, avoiding contents that have settled
and check-out clerks who ask, "Will this be all?"

The years flip backwards, indecipherable
as journal pages from that honeymoon
to Greece—she's forgotten her shorthand.
What she remembers now are the requests,
the favorite birthday dinners of each child,
the man she fed for thirty years who loved her
mashed potatoes, who walked out one day.
She's kept his dinner warm for seven months,
her fingers thinning, wedding band so loose
it falls into the angelfood cake batter.

Madame L. Describes the Siege of Paris

You say that you could never eat a snake?
Had you been here, mademoiselle, in seventy-one
this zoo would seem the freshest of buffets.
We too would have denied it of ourselves
but war is turpentine that strips the gloss.

We built a wall to keep the Prussians out
and barricaded Haussmann's boulevards.
We forged new guns, drilled soldiers for attack,
then waited for the shells. They never hit.
Too late we learned they meant to starve us out.
It seemed almost a joke those first few days,
our handsome soldiers yawning, playing chess.
When Bismarck sneered, "The Paris bourgeoisie
will break after a day without eclairs,"
we laughed. Then had a day without eclairs.
The jokes, and children, thinned. The markets stalled—
we lost our fruit. We lost the beef and eggs.
Stale bread and unripe camembert were hawked
for sums—Mon Dieu—that tripled overnight.
The first milk-hungry babies made their moans.
Flaubert bought braces, his first pair in years—
his belly couldn't hold his trousers up.
We thought it'd gotten bad. Then it got worse.
The *ville des lumières* went out—no light!
No oil for lamps, no coal to feed the stoves.
November, and too cold to sit inside.
The poor huddled along the Champs Élysées,
mobbed kiosks, tore up cherry trees for wood.
At café tables, men ceased their debate
on art and God—they only spoke of food.
And they got drunk and drunker—we had wine
and mustard in abundance all those months.

I was young like you and had a man,
an officer, but stationed in Angers.
The tracks were cut. Although I dreamt of him
and how he'd feed me *beurre et sucre crêpes*,
the weeks grew long. Soon I just dreamt of *crêpes*.
The plump girl he had loved discovered ribs
and collarbones and hips beneath her dress—
each day I molted memories like a snake.
I knew a boy named Jacques who hunted crows
inside the Tuilleries—I dug for root
of dahlia, and we would picnic there.
Sometimes he put his hands inside my blouse,
a different kind of hunger. Afterwards
he'd tell how he would feed me if he could
madeleines and berries dipped in cream,
gorging me with words til I was full.

The hundredth day of siege: I queued for bread
while baby coffins circled Père Lachaise
like white ants choosing their last picnic spot.
A claustrophobic humor reigned the streets.
We all were single-minded—food—so speech
became superfluous, the same ideas
in every house. The cats, suspicious, felt
in stroking hands the butchers' greedy thumbs
appraising *embonpoint*. The dogs were dumb.
Meows and barks soon came from butchers' carts.
I ate a slice of Siamese at Maude's
that tasted just like chicken with her sauce;
the meatballs made of mice caused Maude to toast:
"To enemies made friends in cooking pots!"
Victor, my dog, was old; though it was *triste*
to fatten him for Christmas, what a roast!
A good dog, Victor, til the very end.

With Paris circumscribed, why keep a horse?
My father used his cane to beat the mob

which tried to steal his mare, but acquiesced
to mother's frank "She's starving; why should we?"
The butcher stayed for *filet de cheval*
and courted me with ham. The town dehorsed.
The soldiers used their strategy on rats;
they baited lines with wax and fished in sewers.
But we ran out of rats. The city paused—
no howl, no cheep, no whinny in the streets—
and panicked. We turned upon the zoo inside
our zoo. Trumpetings and ape-cries from the ark:
the hippopotamus, the kangaroo,
wapiti, bear, and wolf—all mustard-doomed.
We killed them two by two. We cheered the boys
who drove the weeping zoo keeper away
and broke the locks made strong to keep us safe.
On fire, we roasted camel on a spit,
danced palm to bloody palm. The drinking troughs
were filled with wine. Two elephants, the pride
of town, Castor and Pollux, their trunks were sliced,
went writhing in the dirt. My torch shed light
on twins who fed each other bites of ape,
a man who wore moose antlers like a hat,
some boys who worked a bar loose for albino
koala skewers. While at the lion's cage
I felt a hand slip underneath my skirt.
Beard on my neck. Feathers and bones
were all we left to greet the stricken sun.
I threw that dress away, it was so stained.

Later that week Thiers proclaimed defeat,
ceded Alsace-Lorraine, our francs, our pride.
The walls came down and Paris could reworld.
The Brits sent mutton, pies, and currant jam.
And things returned to normal. Shelves restocked.
The butcher shop on Faubourg Saint-Germain
took down its rhino horns. And gardens grew.
Resuming lives, we fought amongst ourselves

a civil war—well, who would govern now?
Who pay the money owed? Who seek revenge?
We were reminded who was rich, who poor,
and so if the poor starved, they could be blamed.

Well, that was years ago. Since then I've seen
more war—called "Great"—if what they say is true,
we'll see another here before too long.
I've stockpiled tins of flour, sugar, grain.
I eat well always now, though it seems bland.
Perhaps because I'm old. Perhaps because
I've nibbled lion from a stranger's lips.
So me, I've settled down, bought Victor Deux.
I plumped up, took a husband and his cares.
My life grew dense: I bore him seven sons.
The four who live prepare themselves to fight
the grandsons of the ones my husband fought.
Jean—that was his name—is gone. I spend
my days on this bench in this zoo. I like
to watch the animals and think of things
and people I have known. It's strange how fresh
the siege is in my mind, as if my life's composed
of those eight months. I think we keep ourselves
so tightly wound we never see our spools.
We saw them, clear as skeletons, that time.
What's wrong? What's right? To live was right. To know
that you could take the heart and eat it raw.

III. The Room of Paper Walls

"Yet she again stood before the notebooks, letting her hand with the stylo in it (which looked, with its fragile entrails showing, like a sea-animal, a sea horse) wait above first one, then another, to let the nature of the 'illumination' decide for itself where it should be written; but the four notebooks, with their various sub-divisions and categories, remained as they were, and Anna laid down her pen."

—Doris Lessing, *The Golden Notebook*

From L' Hôtel Terminus Notebooks

Prologue: Holding an Open House

I sing of the millennium, the most misspelled word of the mil-
    lennium.

I sing of the four categories from which art is drawn:
                              ambition, love, religion, and death.
(This according to a former biologist, prone to classification,
but a man who said, "The most beautiful part of my wife is the
scar where her breast used to be." See? You believe him too).
    —Mr. Daylater: Who, me?
    —Yes, you.
    —Mr. Daylater: I don't believe I do.

These are notes toward a poem without narrative structure, or
structure only inferred through classification.
    —Mr. Daylater: This won't work, you know. We're
    enthralled by the linear. It's our destiny.

William Matthews, in his writing journal:
"How private is a journal if some entries get published? Who's
this written for? What does it mean to sing in the shower? If a
shower falls over on a desert island . . .?"

Stephen Dunn:
"The journal is offered in the spirit of someone open and vain
enough to let you in his house. It's possible that a part of him
always had you in mind."
    —Mr. Daylater: You got the vanity part alright.

- A poem like Larry Rivers' "Double Portrait of Berdie," where
  preliminary sketches aren't painted over—the model has
  been tested in different positions.
- A poem with cross-outs; everybody would read different

words, different poems, a palimpsest—
   —Mr. Daylater: Don't you use no fancy words, girl
   —Why can Bob Dylan record a song ten different
ways, expanding and cutting it, changing the tempo
and tone, poking fun at himself even, but a published
poem is locked, historical? I think—
   —Mr. Daylater: Using qualifiers like "I think" is a
mark of female speech. You lack assertiveness, or
want people to think you do.
   —Well—
   —Fillers are feminine too.
   —

- A poem that rehabilitates the exclamation mark!
- A poem with an analogue for the personal, a la Glück's
  Meadowlands.

   —Mr. D: Remember how in speech class long ago
you were told if you were nervous to imagine your
audience in their underwear?
   —So?
   — Mr. D: Well, that was only fair. They're imagining
you in yours.
   —Stop it.
   —Mr. D: If your students read your poems, it's for
gossip.
   —No & Im not listening
   —Mr. D: The critics massacred *Meadowlands*. Too
personal.
   —No I'm plugging my ears & singing Frère Jacque
   —Mr. D: What color are your panties?
   —I'm writing To begin:

I. Ambition, or the Will to Power

I sing of neologisms, the ugliness of neologisms:
the tennis player who possessed not tenacity but "stick-to-it-
    ive-ness";
the church singles seminar on Reboundation;
Kinko's, which is a whole new way to office.

Ambition and Science:
1) Genes from the lobster are being bred with the strawberry
   so it resists cold.
2) Flavor specialists can duplicate all tastes but three: coffee,
   bread, and chocolate.
3) Evolutionary biologists study the new male "bold guppy,"
   which gets eaten because it taunts its bass predators.
   Although bold guppies die young, the trait gets passed on
   because females prefer bold mates. Cross reference with
   "Love/Sex."

A parable about ambition:

For hundreds of years, explorers had hoped to find
Ubar, the lost city of Arabia buried by sand. It had been fabu-
lously rich because it was surrounded by a forest of valuable
frankincense trees, which were used in embalming and sacri-
fices. It had been fabulously wicked because it was fabulously
rich.

It was thought that the key to finding the buried city
would be finding the buried road, which, due to the frankin-
cense trade, would have been well traveled. The explorers
searched X-rays taken by the space shuttle for a line of dense,
packed sand. Finally, the shuttle's ninety-first orbit of earth
revealed such a line, and the explorers tore across the desert in
jeeps. But much gets lost in the desert, and they couldn't find
the road. Eventually they reached a dingy city of patched tents.
The people living there knew nothing about the lost city. The
explorers set up camp and searched outward in spokes.

Nothing. Finally, as they packed to leave, an intern found beneath their camp the ruins of a stadium two thousand years old. They had been sleeping in the lost city of Ubar.

- The city forgot itself. Frankincense fell out of style? Then some mother forgot to say, "Kids, this dump used to be Ubar." Then another. And soon, no one alive remembered. Connect this to how Tommy doesn't know his nationality.

- Or skip the story and link to www.pbs.org. Erasure of the artist. Fractioning of authority.

> —Don't you get booksmart on me, babe.
> —Don't you tell me don't

I love the ghostly dotted lines on Nevada maps, place markers for where the lakes would be if they had water.

Elizabeth Bishop carried lists of conversation topics when she met Marianne Moore: "Mutual Friends," "Favorite Poems," "Strange Animals I Have Known."

We couldn't make rent one April in grad school so Tommy got a job with Pizza Hut, which had one criterion for its drivers— no facial hair. We shaved him and I kissed his naked cheeks. They were hot and pink. He put on the stiff red baseball cap and slowly left for work. I remembered how my long-haired terrier would be embarrassed for a day or two after being shaved for summer and wouldn't go outside.

Frank Lloyd Wright, when asked what his best building was:
"The next one."

Ambition and art:
When Michelangelo's statue of Moses, one of his last, was unveiled, Michelangelo attacked it, beating it with his fists and screaming, "Why aren't you alive? Speak!"

Ambition and error:
In the Old Testament, Moses has light beams shining from his head, but Michelango's Moses has horns, a mistranslation of the Hebrew word for "light."

Ambition satisfied too late:
Michelangelo was paid thirty-six flasks of Trebbiano wine, but his friends were all dead. To the delivery boy: "Who will I drink it with?"

• Moses never reached the promised land but led others close. Michelangelo also never reached his promised land (sculpture so real it becomes human) but led others close. Connect this?

On downsizing:
New technology has allowed astronomers a closer look at Pluto. It's much smaller than previously thought—only 1,400 miles in diameter. It's not solid—it's an amalgam of ice and rock in a field with other such bodies. And its orbit is elliptical and highly erratic. In short, it's not really a planet at all. But some scientists don't want Pluto demoted; it would confuse the public, it's the only "American" planet, and NASA would stop funding the Pluto express. Others are voting for accuracy, backed of course by textbook companies, eager to publish revised editions.

Ambition among friends:
T. S. Eliot, in what passed for a favorable review:
"Miss Moore takes great pleasure in wiping soiled words clean."
        —Mr. D: I believe you mean "between friends."

Mr. Daylater's Advice on Ambition

Never admit to it.
Never say, "I've got words
of a higher wattage,
stand back, I'll screw
them in." Never say,
"You'll need a towel
around your hand, baby,
just to turn the page."
Instead, say "gosh" and "luck."
Otherwise, they'll crush you
under their boot heels
at someone else's wedding.

I buy a used dictionary and find underlined:
> man•qué \ män-kā´\ adj. (F. fr. pp. of *manquer,* to
> lack, fail, fr. It. *mancare* fr. *manco* lacking, left-hand-
> ed, fr. L. having a crippled hand, prob. from *manus.*
> 1778): short of or frustrated in the fulfillment of one's
> aspirations or talents—used postpositively <a poet ~>

Ambition:
root word,
        "bite,"
from the Latin,
        "to be bitten
        when one desires sleep,
        to be gnawed in the dark,
        especially after a night of flirting and wine."
Or from the French,
        "The calendar, it taunts one."
As in:
        "It is wearisome when the priestess
        forbids entrance to the inner circle
        & one is always knocking at her head."

See: <a poet ~>
See you sing it to the tune of "Yes, We Have No Ambition."

"I've seen ambition without understanding
                              in a variety of forms" —
I've seen one fat bumblebee
    chase six hummingbirds from their crimson sugar water.

Living in this Apartment Building without Tommy, Pt. I:
    The Essential Loneliness of Art

              The pet shop owner
              only guarantees song
         from birds kept in separate cages.

Ambition and racism:
Miles Davis being beaten up outside a club for walking a white
woman to her car. Davis pointed to his name on the mar-
quee — "Don't you know who I am?" — for that, they beat him
harder.

From My Seamstress, Marie, in the Power Outage during My
              Bridesmaid Gown Fitting:

       World War II hadn't reached the tiny Austrian village
where Marie lived as a girl, but it was about to. Because they
lived high in the mountains and because no Jews lived there,
they had seen nothing. They had heard stories, they weren't
sure what to make of them, they decided to hide. Marie and
her family joined thirty others in an abandoned wine cellar
concealed on the mountainside. They stayed there for many
days, occasionally sending out a scout at night. This was how
they learned the war was over. The war was over! The war was
over, and the Russians had come to liberate the people. In the

wine cellar, they discussed whether they should leave. They still had water, candles, dried fish, jars of beets and cabbage and strawberry jam.

There were two other girls in the shelter about Marie's age. She knew them from school—they were silly, plump, and pretty—and they were yearning to leave. They were tired of the dirt and the damp. And they were curious, giggled in the dark about the Russian soldiers. But the families voted to stay.

That night Marie woke and saw the girls had lit candles and were pulling silk dresses from their satchels. Plaiting each other's hair. Washing their faces with the drinking water.

At dawn, two Russian soldiers entered the shelter and the first thing they did was rape the girls in silk dresses. Then they lit candles and looked over the families, opened the parcels, and they took the silver and took the jewelry. When the soldiers held candles up to Marie's mud-streaked face, she pressed the strawberry jam on her tongue through her teeth. So, because she was clearly a dirty, syphilitic whore, they went back and raped her two classmates for a while longer.

—Enough about ambition, I think.

II. Love/Sex

I sing of writers who married other writers and are still married.
    —Mr. Daylater: This is going to be a short section.

I sing of Tommy's typo: "I live you."
    —Mr. D: Tell them about your father.

I had a dream in which Tommy—
    —Mr. D: It's strange that you rarely write about your
    father. What about that assignment you give your stu-
    dents: "Write about what terrifies you"?

I'll tell you this: when I was a girl and fell asleep in the car,
he'd carry me into our house to keep me from waking.
When I was a girl and sick he'd bring me rainbow sherbet and
coloring books.
When I was a girl he'd take my sister and me to his office. We'd
be in matching dresses and he'd let us fill our pockets (they
were appliqued with apples) with as many colored pens from
his desk as we wanted.
When I was a girl he would buy me a candy bar each Sunday
after church.
    —Mr. D: Tell them about now.

When I was fifteen and learning to drive he'd stand in the
driveway and flag his arms like he was coaching a pilot down a
runway. When I was a girl—
    —Tell them.
What, Mr. D?
    —Throw them a bone. One of your own.
When he left us, my mother made me sleep on father's old side
    of the bed.
    —And now?
Now? I don't think about it much, during the day.
    —And at night?
My sister wears a mouth guard because she grinds her grief.

—And you?

Tommy hears me call out "Daddy?" in my sleep.

    —Go on.

No. There's too much written already about this kind of shit.

    —How coy, affecting boredom with the confessional,
    when really you lack the guts.

I just don't see the point, Daylater.

    —The point, B. A., is would it be good in a poem?

Okay. Would it be good in a poem?

    —No.

Enough about love, I think.

Let's talk about sexy:

Alison A. who kept dried bear scat on her bookcase.

The surprise of a muskmelon bellying through where the last
    tenant's garden had been.

The moist breath of a horse on your arm hair.

Nai returning to Lebanon for her arranged marriage, unscarf-
    ing her black mane for her husband on their wedding
    night. I lived with Tommy three years before our wed-
    ding—and no man had seen Nai's hair.

Saturday evenings in college, drinking a beer in the dorm
    showers. Denise, Beth, Carmen, and I would shout over
    the water about where we'd go, what we'd borrow to wear.
    And later, standing behind Denise and fastening her bra
    because she'd dislocated her shoulder in soccer.

    —Mr. D: Oooooh, do tell. I luv chik-on-chik stories.

    —No, I'm entirely serious. That intimacy—I miss it.
    We used to nap on Sundays in the Papasan, curled
    like puppies.

• For a poem about touch:

1. A baby who is fed but not touched will die.

2. Waitresses who touch their patrons get better tips.

3. Sociologists observing teenagers say:

    a. Parisian teens touch each other more, but

b. American teens touch themselves, fiddling with rings, cracking knuckles.

But we're threatened by contact. Because we identify with our cars? And even our computers get viruses.

(Intimacy linked to pain—I covered my eighth-grade hickeys with curling iron burns.)

> —Mr. Daylater: Your idea to compare Moses and Michelangelo?
> —Yeah?
> —It'd never work. Metaphor too unwieldy.
> —Piss off, Daylater.
> —You never told us about your panties.

From some wanker on the cruise ship during our honeymoon:
"Come on, baby, this is maritime, not married time. International law don't apply out here."

I had a pocket of *forints* but not enough to exchange so before my train left Budapest I visited the market by Liberty Bridge. At noon, when the other passengers spread their handkerchiefs to eat, I unwrapped bread braided with caraway seeds, a creamy cheese veined with dill, shaved salami, a few kinds of pickles, a red bell pepper, a bag of almonds roasted with paprika. The woman across from me leaned forward. I gestured at my food. She shook her head. I held out my palm crossed with squares of bitter chocolate, cresents of clementines. She shook her head again. She pursed her lips, warming up, wanting to say something. "You laugh yourself," I heard. And then I realized she said, "love."

> —Mr. Daylater: You sometimes sound a little self-congratulatory.

Park City, Utah:
A table full of writers. As the waitress put down the chips and
salsa, I said I love Mexican restaurants because they feed you
immediately. Rodney Jones leaned forward and said, "You've
got the soul of a fat woman." I took offense, which means it's
true.

> —Mr. Daylater: Will you change the names, B. A.? I
> bet you'll change the names. Pathetic, your need to
> be liked.

Sex and the state I'm probably moving to:
Alabama has outlawed vibrators.

> Living in This Apartment Building without Tommy,
> Pt. II

> Rob and Sheila stroll down the walk.
> Light clings to them, a sticky residue.
> I know their names only from the way
> they call out in the night. I imagine
> the cross section of this building,
> a backless doll house: them upstairs,
> legs of their jeans twined beside the bed,
> me at this desk or lying down with my fingers
> again, calling out when she does.

Zoologists were trying to breed a rare female rhino that had
never given birth. Every time they shipped in a mate, she
bucked him off with her horn. Growing frustrated, the zoolo-
gists drugged her, tied her down, and sawed off her horn. So
then she couldn't fight the male off any more. But still she
never conceived.

The *Harlequin* guidelines for authors stipulate that the heroine
must not have a college degree. Copy and paste to "ambition."

My ex-boyfriend saying suspiciously,
"B. A., there are a lot of parades in your poetry."

Bumping into Him After the Breakup

Having shouldered far into the cool, blue forest
I recollect I left the oven on.

Nature and Whether Humans are Designed for Fidelity

In animals that mate for life, the two sexes look so alike as to be indistinguishable to humans—think of Canadian geese and California field moles. Monogamous animals choose mates on basis of their personalities, and they share duties and jointly raise the young. Over time, the wiring of their brains grows more alike.

Polygamous animals choose mates on basis of physical features, especially ones that signify sexual prowess. The male and female of the species can be easily told apart, and in general, the more distinct they look, the more mates they have, and the more strict their division of labor. For example, the bright red male cardinal doesn't care for his young because he'd attract predators to the nest.

Men and women only look eighty percent alike.

Speaking disparagingly
of my disengaged speaker—
"Reveal yourself more,"
said Professor Amphibrach
sounding vaguely lewd
with his office door shut—
I tend to agree with Fulton—
"The priming is a negligee. . .
the canvas needs more veil."

And Klimt, those gold
brocades he paved,
his women swimming
in patterned robes
up to their lobes—
he died, "The Bride" undone,
exposed—he'd paint
his virgins bare,
legs spread, much hair,
each curl detailed,
such fine-tipped strokes—
"beyond anything required
to create an underlying
structure for the fabric"—
then—zip—a cover up,
a wet T-shirt
for him to judge—
Don't touch—
in thick gilt wash—
"for his private
erotic gratification."

My friend in the book biz saying
         female poets' jacket photos are getting larger.

My friend in urban planning saying
         the garage is now the focal point of the home.

         —Mr. Daylater: You have a lot of friends. Some of
         whom even exist.

I worry for my friends.

My friends aren't well.
No not at all.
Elaine sells candles at the mall.

I have seen the best minds of my generation
subsist on Ramen noodles, 3/$1.00,
and I have seen the man who invented Charlie the Tuna
buy a round for the house
and toast, "Screw the dolphins."

Reading Comprehension: Discern the Main Point

In Africa, the male bowerbird builds a bower on the forest floor out of sticks. Then, to attract a female, he decorates his bower. He weaves bright flower petals into the framework and even creates a path to his door with red berries and irides-cent blue beetle wings. When she arrives, he dances for her, sometimes with a blossom in his beak.

Inside, he mates with her so violently it damages his bower. When he's finished, he drives her away. The female, sometimes severely wounded, flies away, if she can, to build a nest where, unprotected, she'll raise the young alone. Although the male doesn't mate again that season, he repairs his bower, replaces wilted blooms and rearranges colored pebbles.

Why do scientists study the bowerbird? _____

_____

No. They do not study it to understand the cruelty in the mat-ing. They study it because, even after the mating instinct has passed, the male still seems to appreciate art.

III. Religion

I sing of a section that is hypothetical.
I sing of a section that is hypocritical.
I sing of a section that knows when you're alone in your
house.

Make Money at Home!
Be a Professional Artist!
To see if YOU have TALENT
sketch God here:

A priest, a rabbi, and a minister walk into a bar together.
"What is this," the bartender says, "some kind of joke?"

July 16, 1999, Arkansas

   M. and I sit on the listing porch of a cabin he built in
the Ozarks with lumber from a demolished church. We drink
beers as the dark strolls in. From the woods we hear a moan.
M. tells me the "Vision Questers" are here for their retreat.
Each quester is isolated in the woods by the medicine man who
pierces him under the collarbones, threads a spike under the
muscle on each side, and ropes the ends of the spikes to trees.
The quester leans into that harness of pain until the spikes
break from his weight. This takes days, days when the visions
come.
   They are fools to love a god who loves their grief? I
suppose. But what have we gained by loving a god who would
spare us? Who can blame a man who wants a scar over his
heart like a seductive zipper? I knew several years ago M. had
gone that route. The chewing-the-cactus buds, sweating-in-the-
lodge route. And M. is a good person, he knew it was bullshit
that menstruating women are barred from the sweat lodge. He
played the guitar. He played the guitar the way a woman wants
to be played to. I had kissed him a few times.

—Mr. D: You did a bit more than that, if I recall.

From the bum in the bus station:
"I'm Jesus Christ, Son of Man, and I need a buck-fifty to get
    to South Jersey."

Because the Dutch had no royalty, and because
Calvinism forbid religious subjects, Dutch artists turned to
everyday scenes. As a result, we have Vermeer's "Woman
Writing a Letter."
    Because Theophilus convinced the twelfth century to
"to subdue Sloth by Embellishing the House of God," we have:
    1) a bone comb with foot-long tines for the priest's hair;
    2) a rubied drinking straw for Christ's blood;
    3) a flabella of ivory and pearl to fan flies from the altar.

Religion and Nostalgia

    Lately I've been thinking about my waitressing years,
which proves one can be nostalgic for anything. There were
seven of them, high school through college, and I don't
remember a single night clearly. They all began with the sea-
lit calm at the start of the shift, me at the hostess station tying
my long white apron around my waist while studying the chart
of tables divided into sections. This was followed by several
hours of pure adrenaline. Then a few hours on the bar stool at
the local, in my trouser pocket a wad of dollars curled around
my black bow tie. If I skipped the drinks and went home, I'd
spin into nightmares where I'd wait on that night's tables again,
but the London Broil was eighty-sixed and me in the weeds
with a new six-top, table 103 needing water but the bus boys in
the walk-in snorting gas from the whip cream canister.
    I think I thought God would saunter in one day and
grab my ass, take me to his pad and play me bootleg B-sides,
give me hickies, work my bra clasp with his ear against my
chest like a safe cracker. You're the man. Come and be my

cupid, stupid, let me be your bitch du jour. I got a nice snack tray, Lord, we're talking serious tatas. I'm in the weeds for real now, Lord, come save me from my penguin suit, I'm here.

      I got out of waitressing just in time, and while my job now is more fulfilling, I'm not half so expert at it. And somewhere along the way, I stopped holding my watch to my ear. Anybody this late isn't coming.

Frank Lloyd Wright built three right turns into the entrance to his Unity Temple. He forces you to slow down to be ready for prayer.

The angel angle:
Why do we turn to other worlds when we have something angelic in ourselves? My legs in the marathon when I'd been running so long I'd forgotten them and looked down—what marvelous machines! And they are mine.
Think of Berryman writing of Bradstreet giving birth: "I did it with my body."
That is how we understand: simple words. Our best insights come in phrases so basic we'd be ashamed to share them. (When we try anyway—cross reference under "Love").
      —Mr. D: I like how you slipped in that you ran a marathon.
      —It's a telling detail, Daylater.
      —It's a bragging detail, B. A.
The only angel I want—from Paul Klee's sketch, "Spirit Brings a Small Breakfast, Angel Gives Us What We Need." The angel tiptoeing up the stairs, balancing a tray. Maybe every morning we are visited with that solicitude.
      —Mr. Daylater: Think about what you're saying!
      —It can be that way.
      —Was it that way for your friend _____? Your friend _____ who burned a pie and propped open her kitchen door with a brick which let in the man who used the brick on her? "Colonel Criminal with the brick in the kitchen"?

—Stop it Im not listening Im singing Frère Jacque

TO SEARCH THE SYSTEM
>(Hint: "swim" retrieves "swim"
                                 "swim?" retrieves "swim,
                                 swimmer, swimming," etc.)
>Search: "god?"
>Retrieve: "god, gods, goddess, god-like"
>Limit with key phrase: "god? have pity on us?
>Press "Submit"   "Submit"

Ah, mon sobersides, ma soeur,
how much easier to believe in a god
who'd come in crème brûlée,
in rack of lamb, or even
my mother's chili—not this flat bread
that sticks to my ribs like a nail

        —Mr. Daylater: B. A., what about _____?

    It was a beautiful day
    In that land far away
    Where my friend baked a red rhubarb pie.

    She cooked it just right,
    The crust flaky and light,
    The filling sweet, steaming, and high,

    Then she sat down and ate
    Right from the pie plate
    And said, "What a good girl am I!"

Remember the documentary of Jackson Pollock dancing and
dripping over his canvas, while his slim wife looked on from a
stool, smoking and wagging her sandal? But toward the end of

his life, he lost faith. He took up booze again, and took up girls again. Forsaking all his innovation, he even took up the brush again. This ended as it often does: very, very badly. The only question was whether he had a little free will or none. Remember those last paintings, compadres? Those thick, apologetic, godless strokes?

> she burnt the pie she took the brick she propped
> open the door

Esta tarde llueve como nunca; y no
  tengo ganas de vivir, corazon.

Esta tarde es dulce. Por que no ha de ser?
  Viste gracia y pena; viste de mujer.
                    (Cesar Vallejo, "Heces," 1918)

(1) It rains this afternoon as it never did before and I
  (2) do not wish to live [do not feel like going on living],
        [O][my] heart.

(3) This is a gentle [sweet] afternoon. Why not [should it not
        be]?
  (4) It is dressed in grace [humor] and grief [pain][worth];
        dressed like a woman.

On organized religion:
The man walking his dog in the apartment's courtyard,
yelling "Shame!" every time it defecates.

On recovering from organized religion:
With Liz H., talking about remembering our right from left.
Me saying I know by starting to make the sign of the cross.
Her saying she knows by which thumb she used to suck. Me
saying these are the same. Her not saying anything to me for a
long time after.

IV. Death

I sing of a section—
    —Mr. Daylater: where I step out for a smoke.

Ways of dying:
1) The girls in Japan no longer learn how to tie kimonos. Also, the young now refuse to slurp their noodles, though slurping has always been considered a compliment to the chef.

2) The French fear for the baguette now that Monoprix sells Wonder.

3) In the Czech Republic, visiting a man who'd published *samizdat* during Communist censorship. He spoke of the dangers of distributing the stories and poems once they'd been printed. The man's daughter was coloring on the floor. "Dad," she said, "why didn't you just call the people to come get them?" Already forgetting the time, only a few years past, when their phone had been tapped.

4) On the flight to Tucson: the cartographer sent to map Apache land was frustrated. "See?" he asked, pointing to the map across our laps. "What I rename 'Route A'—some Apaches called it 'Trail Goes Down between Two Hills,' and others 'Whiteness Spreads Out Descending to Water,' and still others, 'Juniper Tree Stands Alone.'"

My friend the journalist writes obituaries for the nearly dead. He has hundreds on file, mostly actors and politicians, and when they die he adds the date and closes the parentheses. It makes him happy in a way his wife never could.

My friend the policeman says when they fish drowned men out of the river, they often have their flies open—they'd been pissing when they'd fallen in.

My friend who studies urban legends says they used to be fantastic—the Candyman would kill you if you said his name three times to a mirror. Now, emails circulate saying don't fish in the coin-return on phones, because people stick AIDS-infected needles there, with notes: "Welcome to the real world." Some versions take on a racist slant: Arabs or Germans plant the needles.

Aug. 22, 1998, Madrid Bullfights

It's strange to see one that doesn't want to fight, but the third bull to enter the ring whips around and paws at the gate. Although the picadors poke it, although its balls are in a noose, it bellows and paws. The crowd hisses and throws hazelnuts. Finally the gate opens and the bull is replaced.

That night, sunburned in a café, Kathleen and I eat olives and manchengo cheese and drink wine from a jug. We're trying to talk ourselves into how we feel. The wine is working. We drink to each dead bull and to the third that lives. How un-male: to pass up the glory and goading for a quiet green death back on the farm. But a man comes over to say that it won't live. No, most certainly not. A cautious bull is no good. A cautious bull might spread the fear.

He tells us that he ran with the bulls as a young man and was throttled by the fear. He flattened himself into a doorway to let the bulls roar by. Then he jogged after them in the thunderous silence. He saw, half buried in the mud, a new set of teeth, so he put them on a window ledge in case the owner should return. He trotted on to hear the outcome of the run.

Near the end, he saw the medics standing in a slick of blood, bent over a man still wearing the bull runner's red kerchief. He was holding the two halves of his rib cage closed. His wife was weeping. The man's last words: "Where in Christ's name are my teeth?"

Mona Webb Dies at 94: A Found Poem from *The Willy Street News*

Mona Boulware Webb whose sometimes
shocking art lent color to Willy Street died
Saturday after a stroke. Even those
who didn't know her knew the outside
of her gallery, the Way House of Light,
with its cresent moon mirror mosaic.
Webb lived on the second floor.
Her favorite medium was alabaster.
Although bed-ridden, Webb still created,
said her daughter Cookie. "She made
a mess of her bed. Buttons, sequins, teacups
all glued to the sheets." Despite her diabetes
and numb toes and feet, Webb refused
to move to a nursing home. "And that,"
said Cookie, "was that. But this last year
she didn't do well." Webb is survived
by five children, fifteen grandchildren,
and thirty-six great-grandchildren. They will sort
through her art, which did not sell.

Katrina speaking, with her niece in the room, of watching
    Tim die:
    "And when I turned around from the sink, he was
        gone."
    "Oh," said the girl, "did you look everywhere? In the
        closet? Under the bed?"

In a lobster trap, the net that snags the lobster is called "the parlor." Copy and paste to "Love."

People Trying to Get a Handle on Death

People trying to get a handle on death remind me of Roy and Janet's wonderfully stupid border collie. Roy and Janet would take Tommy and me back to their place after the bars closed. The four of us would walk their dog and it was the same every time. Always the neighbor had her sprinkler on, one of those swiveling handlebar kinds that shoots out two long ropes of water. And damn if that dumb dog didn't stalk it every time. He'd crouch at the lawn edge and drop to his elbows, advance like a soldier under gunfire. The dog was mostly black but with a white tail. In the dark, it was like a flag waving us in. He was young, that dog, and he'd almost make it by the time the water came his way, almost but not quite, so he'd have to leap back, yowling mournfully. After it had passed, he'd crouch and begin the whole thing over. The dog would go on doing this and the four of us would laugh like idiots until the neighbor's lights came on and we had to walk away, just when we were beginning to think he might get it.

From an English language newspaper in Japan:
"The entire airline crew climbed out on the wing of the burning plane and parachuted safely to their death."

Poetry late at night:
I read "tombstone" where it says "trombone."

After I'm gone:
A long, red hair in the cobweb.

Names are important.
The Moscow Circus is not
The Circus of Moscow.
If you go to Moscow, try
to remember that. At one,

you will see the usual,
men shot from cannons, women
sawed in half. You will think,
"death defying."
                         At the other,
you will see a dancing bear
ribby and piebald with mange.
You will think, "threadbear."
The trapeze artist is wrinkled,
yellow makeup covers bruises
on her thighs. You will check
for the safety net. You do not choose
which circus to attend: you are chosen.

Marianne Moore loved the circus.
Marianne Moore is no more.
If you meet her, try to remember that.
If you read her, you might think,
"death-defying." If you read her,
you might think, "What has she done
for me lately?" If you read her,
you might think, "Some safety net."
You might flip to her photo.
You might think, "She should have worn
makeup." You do not choose
what to think: you are chosen.

Dec. 15, 1998, Max Roach Tribute, 92nd Street Y, New York

He is so old it takes him a long time to shuffle across
the stage to his drums. After a pause between the popping ker-
nels of applause, he begins to play. He plays fast and loose. He
plays on the drums, then on the drum stand, then on the floor.
The audience nods and taps. Except the stick flies out of his
hand. Clatters across the stage and rolls in a semicircle. He
draws another from his tuxedo's inner pocket. He has a bunch,
like the child who sharpens all his pencils before a spelling test.

He starts playing again, shakier, but he picks up speed. He picks up speed and then he really goes to town on those drums. The audience hoots and whistles, which doesn't happen that often with white people. Except he knocks over his music stand. The band keeps playing while the stage hands gather the sheet music. They organize it for him, and he bravely dives back in. Again, the crowd gets into it. It is, after all, a tribute. Except he topples off his stool. The band stutters, stops. He's on his back with his feet in the air, his mended heels grinning at the crowd. The stage hands pick him up and carry him into the wings. The people clap so long their hands hurt.

Each region in Ireland has a distinct pattern for its fisherman
      sweaters.
The sweaters are a great favorite with the tourists.
The patterns originated as a way of telling, when a fisherman
      washed up on shore with his face nibbled off, where
      to send the body.

The five years I've known Katrina, she's been grieving for Tim, dead of AIDS. She used to wear his shirts—the shoulder seams would fall to her tiny elbows. Then one day she shows up in a size four yellow blouse. Grief is like that sometimes: after a long while you can find it no longer fits.

From the Texas Prison Museum, Huntsville, TX:

My Last Meal: Morrow, Jr. J. W. #321 Death Row

1 sm. steak (tender, no bone, no fat, cooked med. rare)
1 order of French fried potatoes (lg. order)
1 order of lg. butter beans (sm. order)

1 order of brown grease gravy (med. order)
some hot biscuits
salt and pepper
lettuce (with dressing)
steak sauce
a sliced onion (small)

dessert: 3 large bananas, sliced
and covered with a pint of whipped chocolate ice
    cream
1 piece of fluffy coconut pie

This is my last meal, and damn it, I want it served hot
on however many plates and bowls it takes to keep
from messing any of it up together, and I want it
served at one o'clock tomorrow afternoon.

—Mr. Daylater, from the hallway: Poetry. It's been
done to death.

• Rework these notes to—

—Mr. Daylater: A poet manqué; got a ring to it.
—Im not listening. Frère Jacque.
—Who was it who said, "The greatest poem is
silence"?
—I cant hear you. Dormez-vous.
—You're running out of notebook space. You're run-
ning out of time.
—Daylater?
—What?
—My panties—
—Yes?
—They're green.

Epilogue: L' Hôtel Terminus

No matter the train
when you reach the station
you'll find L' Hôtel Terminus.
As if tracking you.

"Follow me, follow me":
you will follow a back,
a bald spot, up stairs
to an oddly shaped room,
molding on the one original wall
that says, like people with photos,
"I was once something grand.
Consider me."

You will find strange bedfellows there
on sheets that smell like skin,
like human skin—
and through the four chambers
of your heart you will hear
the cough like a sucker punch
repeating from rooms away,
the woman's moan that could be prayer
or lips at the back of her knee,
the curses of the man who sits
with his flashlight because of the bats,
he swears there are bats,
if he closes his eyes they will come,
and the woman who learns herself
into childhood focusing on her tongue
in her own mouth this time
against her bottom teeth—there—
aspirate in the throat—there—to ask,
Where is the bathroom?
What is your name? Names
are important. Her own is a sound
they don't have in this language.

This ends as it often does.
She's pronounced out of her mind.

You will visit us, traveler,
at L' Hôtel Terminus.
The only question is whether
you have a little free will
or none.
There's a way of finding
despair in this
but also a way of finding
the whole world a metaphor
and us the unlikes
connecting and connecting and
connecting.

I beseech you, find it this way.
I worry for my friends.

So when the timer goes off in your body
breaking into your dream like a clumsy burglar
and you enter the hallway
trying to find the bathroom—
what is the word for *bathroom?*
and the timer goes off in the hall
turning on the dark
and you can't find
the way in, the way out—
well, it's the same for the others.

Yes, it's the same for the others.

Every room is different
but the same.

You don't believe me?
Step off this train you call your life—
you're there.

IV. The Room of Everywhere

And now good-morrow to our waking souls,
Which watch not one another out of fear;
For love, all love of other sights controls,
And makes one little room, an everywhere.

—John Donne, "The Good-Morrow"

The Snake Charmer

On our first drive when you yelled "Snake!"
I braced against the lump
  under your tires;
    the men I've known would swerve across two lanes
    to kill a sunning hognose,

 its harmless rattle lodged inside
my throat. Not you. You stopped
  the car, crouched by
    the snake. Your fingers caught its neck like you'd
    pinch lightning in mid-air. Awed,

 you showed the grotto of its jeweled
and earless head, white-welled
  muscle of mouth,
    round eyes free of venom, mosaic vent
    beneath where excrement

comes out. Far enough from the road
you disarmed each other—
  almost purring,
    it unwound, silk spirals into kudzu,
    then vanished. Since then, more than once,

 love-wracked, you've turned with that same awe:
"How is it you love me
  so much?" Well,
    because you stopped. Because your fingers cup
    my neck, and tenderness rises

 beneath them. Because I'm free
to leave. Open your eyes,
  my charmer: I'm
    still wound around your arm. When the snake loves,
    it's the fiercest kind of love.

Why I Can't Cook for Your Self-Centered Architect Cousin

Because to me a dinner table's like a bed—
without love, it's all appetite and stains. Let's buy
take-out for your cousin, or order pizza—his toppings—

but I can't lift a spatula to serve him what I am.
Instead, invite our favorite misfits over: I'll feed
shaggy Otis who, after filet mignon, raised his plate

and sipped merlot sauce with such pleasure
my ego pardoned his manners. Or I'll call Mimi,
the chubby librarian, who paused over tiramisu—

"I haven't felt so satisfied since . . ." then cried
into its curls of chocolate. Or Randolph might stop by,
who once, celebrating his breakup with the vegetarian,

so packed the purse seine of his wiry body with shrimp
he unbuttoned his jeans and spent the evening
couched, "waiting for the swelling to go down."

Or maybe I'll just cook for us. I'll crush pine nuts
unhinged from the cones' prickly shingles.
I'll whittle the parmesan, and if I grate a knuckle

it's just more of me in my cooking. I'll disrobe
garlic cloves of rosy sheaths, thresh the basil
till moist, and liberate the oil. Then I'll dance

that green joy through the fettuccine, a tumbling,
leggy dish we'll imitate, after dessert.
If my embrace detects the five pounds you win

each year, you will merely seem a generous
portion. And if you bring my hand to your lips
and smell the garlic that lingers, that scents

the sweat you lick from the hollows of my clavicles,
you're tasting the reason that I can't cook
for your cousin—my saucy, my strongly seasoned love.

I Would Like to Go Back as I Am, Now, to You as You Were, Then—

then when you bagged grit at the sandblasting factory,
loading train cars that took as much as they could stand
and got the hell out of lower Alabama, as you dreamed of doing,
watching them rumble North with your haiku on their dusty sides
written with your spit-wet finger, before changing from your
        coveralls
for your night school Literature class, your shame, your hope—

Or back, further, to when your mechanic father gave you
a fixed-up car—what you had asked for all through high school,
except it was the first Japanese car the county had seen, a Toyota,
and when you drove by, the boys called it "the rice burner,"
and the girls—pretty, pious, black-and-white as Dalmatians—
wouldn't get inside of it, so you paid five dollars in your empty car
to watch *Planet of the Apes* at the drive-in alone—

Or back even further to you in your plaid pajamas
sitting up half the humid night because asthma sat on your chest
and crushed no matter how you cried Uncle, so you drew
comic books bulging with muscled heroes until the blue rumble
of logging trucks signaled dawn, and better breathing,
and you could sleep, your chest heaving with its tiny
boy nipples, your legs sticking out with their leg bones—

I have loved you for your shame and for your busted body
which aches for three days after we help friends move,
because for years you were valued, like a donkey,
for how much you could carry on your back. I have loved you
for your freakishness, your exile in that homeland
where you hid your paperbacks, spoke the local language,
rose early and carried a gun if you wanted to walk in the woods.

I would like to go back as I am, now, but not as I was then—
unsure what I was prepped for in my Chicago prep school,
where girls skipped Chem to watch boys play soccer, boys
who pulled in our driveways in Benzes then beeped to have us
        hurry,
I wanted to be one of the thin girls dazzling in their meanness
but learned my tongue's too slow to suck that venom, I needed
to fail before meeting you, before learning myself the lucky one—

I would go back as I am, now, bend over your ribs,
lift the damp V of your pajamas and blow on your neck,
blow a breeze smelling like snow, sounding like somebody
whistling far away—I would go back for a ride in your Toyota,
beat time to your eight track of Styx with my feet on the dash,
we'd cruise the drive-in and park, back row center,
let the girls gawk at the windows gauzy with heat—

I would go back and find you at the simmering factory
and free your wet curls from the clench of your hard hat
and unlace your boots almost lunar with red mud
and unzip your coveralls, a zipper long as lower Alabama—
go back as I am, now, and reach in, and kneel down,
and lick you to life, the life we couldn't know we were heading for,
a timely, lucky life, just beyond the margins of this poem.

Good Work if You Can Get It

Last night, hot July 4th in Tucson's barrio,
I watched fireworks shot from a mountain
with locals who bet how soon the mountain
would catch fire. The mariachi didn't drown
the churn of helicopters waiting to douse
the whole thing: the true finale. In the bleachers,
the cops looked on importantly, shook handfuls
of popcorn like dice into their mouths.
I sat behind a man, maybe one of the 3,000
copper miners laid off today, his baby girl
twisting to me over his shoulder.
He couldn't interest her in the sky flowers
no matter how he called *Mira! Mira! Mira!*

Today, because the crowd's been warmed up,
the monsoons break and the real fireworks begin.
Everyone's been waiting: in the hills, the O'odham
have danced the Round Rainbow. Here, the people
sprint into rain which pelts their upturned palms,
blows the creosote into italics, taunts the dogs
into hurling against their cages. I read a cactus guide
this week and picture the saguaro's shallow roots,
each hair-like thread puffing with purpose,
absorbing a whole year's water, while above ground
sharp pleats expand like an accordion,
or like the fan of the transvestite I surprised
in the bathroom restuffing his dress, confiding
Honey, all men are breast men.

Three weeks here. I've learned the cacti—
not only the saguaro looking like a man
imitating a cactus imitating a man pointing away,
but also the spiky blue agave which yields its heart
to tequila; the barrel cactus that portrays life's ratio:
one blossom, four thousand barbs; and the teddy bear cholla,

70

about which the guidebook bizarrely advises
the solitary hiker: *If a cactus joint attaches itself,*
use two pocket combs as levers to flip it away.

How essential is the desert after rain
which stripped the fat stems of palm trees
now curling on the road like rusted tail pipes.
The ornamental orange trees spilled their cargo—
oranges lay in the sand like in Renoir's circus ring
where the audience tossed them for the sequinned girls
who must have flown fabulously on the trapeze.
The glad girls clutch as many as they can
to their flat chests, and still the oranges stud the ground
like copper ingots. Now, of course—so hard
to picture a time when girls clamored for fruit—
people who see the painting think the oranges
juggling balls. Barely a century old, yet we misread it.
You'd think its viewers would know
most love the work's reward but not the work.

What would those girls think of a woman, newly
wed, who kissed her pretty husband farewell
to come to the desert for a month of work?
A clumsy woman among rain-washed needles
that seem harmless as Q-tips but henna
her shins and arms with petroglyphs as she walks
with her cactus book. In front of the saguaro
she thinks accordion, fan, lampshade, thinks
of napkins she folded those years as a waitress
(napkins pleated into swans, napkins pleated into sailboats),
thinks of the baby Jesus in the San Zavier mission
and how each morning the dark women vie
to change his sequined dress and pleat it carefully
before combing the golden human hair.

What would the circus girls think
if they knew the woman returns to this adobe

to write down these moves as if for a game
called *Connect the Whole World*
and her husband phones: *Are you working?*
I can call back if you're working.
He is the kind of man who says things like
You're not clumsy, you're in touch with your surroundings.
He knows that no matter where they go next
she has lodged in her heart this adobe in the desert
because of work she did within its thick pink walls.
See, the work makes her sentimental, perhaps foolishly so.
She tells him about being passed the tequila,
pouring it down the straw of her throat
after the cops had swaggered away
leaving popcorn in the stands like tiny skulls.
The fireworks were nothing then but smoke
swirling into the night like cream into coffee
and five flames stuttering on the mountain.
She says, *How smooth the tequila tasted, after work.*

To have a man like that, and work as well.
How can she account for it? Mostly she fears
she's raiding happiness from the larder
of her next life, or, just as bad, from someone else's.
But sometimes she thinks it's better to quaff this
(a hexed word) luck, and not chase it immediately
with her usual, that old gulp of guilt. Maybe, she thinks,
she owes it to a sadder self to savor this.
To work, to take the tools of her serious play—
her man, the adobe, the tequila and guidebook,
the spines that want a piece of her which she gives
(call her clumsy, call her affectionate),
the cops, transvestite, the *Mira! Mira! Mira!*—
to gather all these oranges to her chest.

Come to Krakow

I want to return to the city where cobblestones
bob like apples to trip the drunks, where a man
in the Planty Gardens slurred at me some Polish
that I later translated: "You have such exquisite
ankles." I want to return to the square to hear
the clock tower's trumpet, its terrible caesura
marking the time the Tartar's arrow pierced
the trumpeter's throat, precisely not quite twelve
one spring day in 1011. I want to be alarmed.

I know there is someone out there who needs Krakow.
Come with me. Come with me there, where life
is not buffered by habit or ease. Let us be almost
poor again, so simpler things matter. Let us
search for the bakery that opened early the night
I wandered, so lost, so cold. When the baker
presses his bread into our chilled fingers, and it steams,
I will tell you of the freezing crow I held, as a girl,
by Lake Michigan. Let things come to life in our hands.

We will walk past the beer halls, the vendors
of pretzels, the women weaving garlic into wreaths,
the castle cinched with moats. We will walk
past the Capuchin cathedral, the chandeliers built
from bones of monks, where newlyweds duck
flung fistfuls of coins, cheaper to throw than rice.
We will walk followed by gypsy children hawking
their enormous eyes, and flower-sellers melting
into lakes of asters, calling, "What is it you lack?"

Less, now. We are lost, which means we notice
everything. I could have been a dancer, I say, given
half a chance. You say you can't swim, but dream
each night of the ocean. We stop to purchase
directions with our handful of dear words. The cider

seller will not tell, gives instead a steaming amber mug
to share: "Drink, drink." I pirouette around a fountain.
You toss in your watch. When it stops its tick,
you'll make a wish. I'll save for you the last good sip.

Notes

In "The Impossibility of Language," "the Kremlin Mountaineer" with "laughing cockroaches on his top lip" who "rolls the executions on his tongue like berries" are phrases from Osip Mandelstam's poem, "The Stalin Epigram." "This shoe-size in earth with bars around it" is from Mandelstam's "You Took Away All the Oceans and All the Room." Both translations are by Clarence Brown and W. S. Merwin. The quote about the death of Northern Pomo is from "Electronic Era Killing Languages, Linguist Laments at Conference," *Northwest Arkansas Times*, April 6, 1997.

The list of items included in the space probe in "The Insecurities of Great Men,"comes from Carl Sagan's *Murmurs of Earth*.

The title from "The Cup Which My Father Hath Given Me," comes from John 18:11, Jesus in the garden of Gethsemane: "Then Simon Peter having a sword, drew it, and smote the high priest's servant, and cut off his right ear. The servant's name was Malchus. Then said Jesus unto Peter, 'Put up thy sword into the sheath: the cup which my Father hath given me, Shall I not drink it?' Then the band and the captain and officers of the Jews took Jesus, and bound him, and led him away." The quote from Coleridge's diary is taken from Richard Holmes' *Darker Reflections*.

In "Mary Speaks to the Early Visitor at the Laying Out," "Doth God exact Day-labour, light denied?" is from Milton's sonnet, "On His Blindness." "Eyeless in Gaza at the mill with slaves" is from Milton's *Samson Agonistes*.

In "From *L' Hôtel Terminus Notebooks*," the journal excerpts from Stephen Dunn and William Matthews are from *The Poet's Notebook*, ed. by Stephen Kuusisto, Deborah Tall, and David Weiss. The T. S. Eliot quote is from his introduction to

Marianne Moore's *Selected Poems*. "I've seen ambition without understanding in a variety of forms" is from Moore's poem, "Critics and Connoisseurs." "The priming is a negligee ... the canvas needs more veil" is from Alice Fulton's poem, "The Priming Is a Negligee" from her book *Sensual Math*. The information on Klimt is from *The Life and Works of Gustave Klimt* by Nathaniel Harris. "I did it with my body" is from John Berryman's "Homage to Mistress Bradstreet." The Paul Klee sketch is in the Carl Djerassi Room of the San Francisco Museum of Modern Art. Thanks to James Carlos Blake for reading an early version of this poem.

The complete pesto recipe from "Why I Can't Cook for Your Self-Centered Architect Cousin" is 2 c. basil, 3 cloves garlic, 1/4 c. pine nuts, 1/4 c. olive oil, 1/2 c. parmesan cheese, and 1/2 t. salt.

The Renoir painting, *Two Little Circus Girls*, in "Good Work if You Can Get It" is in The Art Institute of Chicago. This painting, like many others, was first introduced to me by my mother.

About the Author

Beth Ann Fennelly is the author of *Unmentionables, Great with Child: Letters to a Young Mother, Tender Hooks*, and *Open House*. Originally published by Zoo Press in 2001, *Open House* won the 2001 *Kenyon Review* Prize and the GLCA New Writers Award, and was a Book Sense Top Ten poetry pick. Poems from the collection later went on to appear in the *Best American Poetry* series and *The Penguin Book of the Sonnet*, and to win a Pushcart Prize.

Fennelly has received fellowships from the National Endowment for the Arts and the Breadloaf Writers' Conference, and she was Diane Middlebrook Fellow at the University of Wisconsin. Currently a professor of English at the University of Mississippi, Fennelly has been awarded a Fulbright scholarship to Brazil. She lives with her husband, the novelist Tom Franklin, and their children in Oxford, Mississippi.